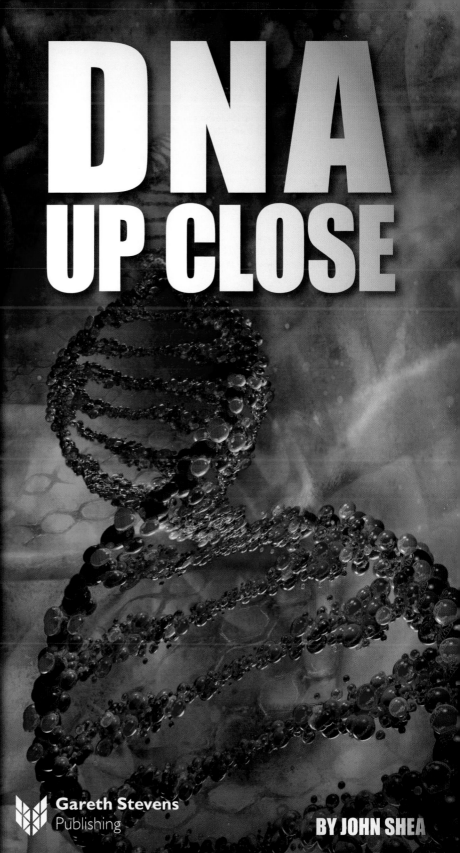

UNDER THE
MICROSCOPE

DNA
UP CLOSE

Gareth Stevens
Publishing

BY JOHN SHEA

Please visit our website, www.garethstevens.com. For a free color catalog of all our high-quality books, call toll free 1-800-542-2595 or fax 1-877-542-2596.

Library of Congress Cataloging-in-Publication Data

Shea, John M.
DNA up close / John M. Shea.
    p. cm. — (Under the microscope)
Includes index.
ISBN 978-1-4339-8343-6 (pbk.)
ISBN 978-1-4339-8344-3 (6-pack)
ISBN 978-1-4339-8342-9 (library binding)
1. DNA—Juvenile literature. I. Title. II. Series: Under the microscope.
QP624.S54 2014
572.8'6—dc23

                                    2012047152

First Edition

Published in 2014 by
Gareth Stevens Publishing
111 East 14th Street, Suite 349
New York, NY 10003

Copyright © 2014 Gareth Stevens Publishing

Designer: Katelyn E. Reynolds
Editor: Therese Shea

Photo credits: Cover, p. 1 Adrian Neal/Lifesize/Thinkstock.com; cover, pp. 1, 3–31 (logo and DNA image icons) iStockphoto/Thinkstock.com; cover, pp. 1–31 (DNA image icon) Jason Reed/Photodisc/Thinkstock.com; cover, pp. 1–31 (DNA image icon) Comstock/ Thinkstock.com; cover, pp. 1–32 (background texture) Hemera/Thinkstock.com; p. 5 Don W. Fawcett/Photo Researchers/Getty Images; p. 7 Comstock/Thinkstock.com; p. 9 Leonard Lessin/Photo Researchers/Getty Images; p. 11 iris 42/Shutterstock.com; p. 12 © iStockphoto.com/amtitus; p. 13 Andreas Feininger/Time & Life Pictures/Getty Images; p. 15 Omikron Omikron/Photo Researchers/Getty Images; p. 16 Laguna Design/Oxford Scientific/Getty Images; p. 17 Alila Sao Mai/Shutterstock.com; p. 19 © iStockphoto.com/ nicolas_; p. 20 Cultura Science/Rafe Swan/Oxford Scientific/Getty Images; p. 21 Joe Raedle/Getty Images; p. 23 BioPhoto Associates/Photo Researchers/Getty Images; p. 25 Jim Dowdalls/Photo Researchers/Getty Images; p. 27 TEK Image/Science Photo Library/ Getty Images; p. 29 iStockphoto/Thinkstock.com.

CONTENTS

The Instructions for Life 4

The Chemistry of Life 6

Chromosomes 8

Unraveling DNA 10

Translating the Genetic Code 14

Learning the Language 18

Genetics and Electron Microscopes 22

Tiny Factories 24

Forensics 26

The Future of Genetics 28

Glossary 30

For More Information 31

Index 32

Words in the glossary appear in **bold** type the first time they are used in the text.

THE INSTRUCTIONS FOR LIFE

The variety of life on this planet is amazing. Giant redwood trees tower in West Coast forests while tiny **bacteria** break down the **nutrients** the trees need to stay alive. The largest animal on Earth, the blue whale, swims over creatures that live so deep in the ocean that sunlight never reaches them.

Despite this variety, all living things share much in common. We're all made of cells, and each cell contains DNA. DNA provides the instructions for life. It tells trees to grow tall and bacteria to grow quickly. It enables whales to grow fins to swim and underwater creatures to find food without the sun. All living things contain DNA, and yet it's DNA that makes each of us special.

4

CELLULAR PIONEERS

Robert Hooke was the first person to use the word "cell" in 1665. As he looked at a piece of cork under a microscope, he saw tiny units. He named them cells because they reminded him of the rooms where monks live, called cells. In 1831, scientist Robert Brown named the central body he saw within a plant cell the "nucleus." Brown's work with plant cells made him think the nucleus was important for cell growth.

Human cells are full of important structures. Perhaps the most important part, however, is the nucleus in each cell, which houses DNA.

nucleus

5

THE CHEMISTRY OF LIFE

DNA stands for deoxyribonucleic (dee-AHK-sih-ry-boh-noo-klee-ihk) acid. It's a very long, very thin strand of molecules called nucleotides. Each nucleotide is made up of three separate molecules: a chemical compound called a phosphate, a sugar called deoxyribose, and another chemical compound called a base. All nucleotides have the same phosphate and sugar. Four different bases are joined to them. These are adenine, thymine, guanine, and cytosine.

Every kind of life on this planet uses the same four nucleotides to make DNA. The nucleotides have long scientific names that tell us what they're made of. Scientists shorten these names to dAMP, dCMP, dGMP, and dTMP. The nucleotides stack on top of each other to form a shape very similar to a ladder that coils around itself. This is called a double helix.

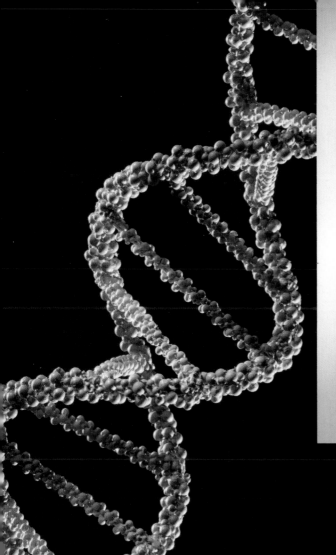

MICROSCOPIC BUT LONG!

DNA is extremely thin and incredibly long. If the DNA from a single human cell were stretched out, it would be about 6 feet (1.8 m) in length. There are over 50 trillion cells in your body. If the DNA from each of your cells were placed end to end, it would be about 62 billion miles (100 billion km) long! That's enough DNA to stretch from Earth to the sun and back again more than 300 times.

You can see how scientists came up with the nucleotides' names on the chart. The double helix is pictured here as well.

BASE	BASE + SUGAR	BASE + SUGAR + PHOSPHATE (NUCLEOTIDE)
adenine (A)	deoxyadenosine	deoxyadenosine monophosphate (dAMP)
thymine (T)	deoxythymidine	deoxythymidine monophosphate (dTMP)
guanine (G)	deoxyguanosine	deoxyguanosine monophosphate (dGMP)
cytosine (C)	deoxycytidine	deoxycytidine monophosphate (dCMP)

7

CHROMOSOMES

In the 1800s, microscopes weren't powerful enough to see DNA. Scientists used dyes that made parts of the cell stand out. This is how German scientist Walther Flemming first found chromosomes in the nucleus. He named them this because they stained well. (The prefix "chromo" means "color.") Flemming watched these structures as cells divided in two. He observed that the chromosomes doubled, and each new cell received half.

Scientists have since learned that chromosomes are actually tightly wrapped packages of DNA. They keep DNA compact enough to fit into cells and make it easier for DNA to be passed to each new cell when dividing. Chromosomes are the structures in which new cells receive information responsible for **traits**.

8

CHROMOSOMES AND INHERITANCE

People have 46 chromosomes, or 23 pairs, in each cell. We inherit 23 of these from our mother, while the other 23 we get from our father. Occasionally, however, some people inherit an extra chromosome. This can result in serious medical problems. Those with Down Syndrome have an extra chromosome 21, which can cause heart problems and learning disabilities. Down Syndrome affects 1 out of 800 babies.

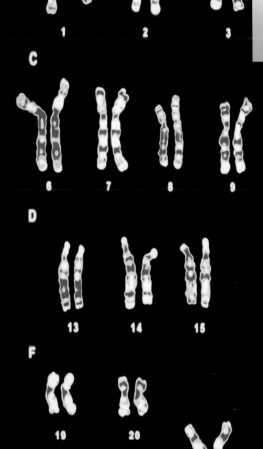

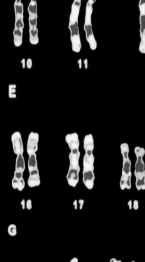

A picture of a person's chromosomes, as seen through a microscope and arranged by size, is known as a karyotype.

9

UNRAVELING DNA

By the first half of the 1900s, most scientists suspected that DNA was important for providing instructions to cells, but they had no idea how it worked. They didn't even know what DNA looked like. The molecules were so small that they couldn't be seen with a regular light microscope. Much of the research into DNA depended on studying its chemical properties.

In 1949, biochemist Erwin Chargaff made an important observation about the bases found in the nucleotides of DNA. He found that in every living thing's DNA the amount of adenine is the same as the amount of thymine. And the amount of guanine is the same as the amount of cytosine. Later, researchers found out that adenine bonds only with thymine in DNA and cytosine bonds only with guanine.

10

MITOCHONDRIAL DNA

While most human DNA is found in the nucleus, there's a tiny amount found in small structures known as mitochondria. Mitochondria are the power plants of the cell. They release energy from food. The mitochondrial DNA provides instructions for making the proteins that the mitochondria need. Plants have structures called chloroplasts to convert the sun's energy to food. They also contain a small amount of DNA.

Structure of DNA
deoxyribonucleic acid

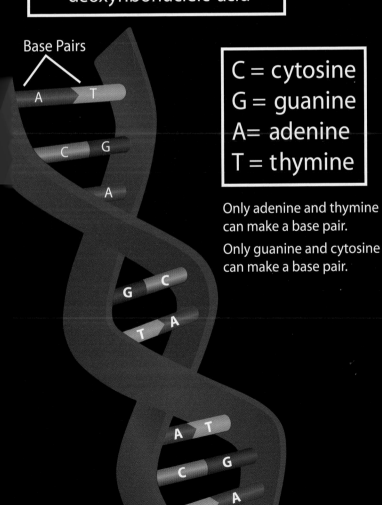

Base Pairs

C = cytosine
G = guanine
A = adenine
T = thymine

Only adenine and thymine can make a base pair.

Only guanine and cytosine can make a base pair.

Chargaff also discovered that human DNA contains about 20 percent each of guanine and cytosine, and about 30 percent each of adenine and thymine.

11

AN UNREWARDED
HERO

Research chemist Rosalind Franklin, working with Maurice Wilkins, approached studying DNA in a new way. She shot **X-rays** at DNA and measured how they bounced off. This helped her mathematically determine the size and shape of DNA. It was her research that suggested DNA was a double helix and led to Watson and Crick's ideas about DNA's bonds. Unfortunately, Franklin died in 1958 at the young age of 37 and didn't get to share the Nobel Prize.

Watson and Crick discovered how the bases of nucleotides bond. This finding suggested what DNA looked like.

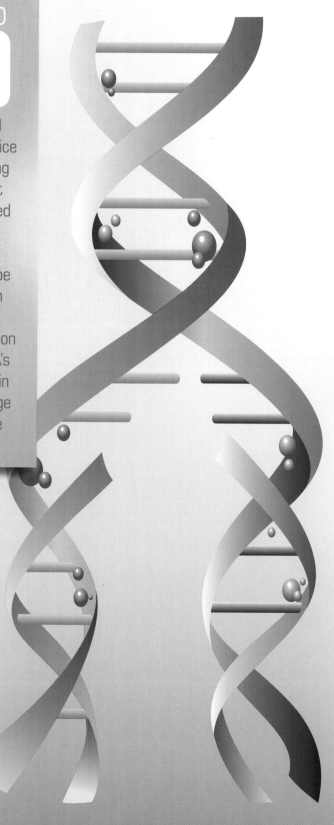

12

Chargaff's work provided an important clue to James Watson and Francis Crick. They suspected what DNA looked like, but they found proof in 1953. They discovered that the bond of the bases adenine and thymine was exactly as long as the bond of cytosine and guanine. These bonds (the "rungs of the ladder") would cause the DNA to curve around itself in a double helix.

In finding out DNA's structure, Watson and Crick also found out how it replicated, or copied, itself. If the bonds between the nucleotides were separated like unzipping a zipper, each strand would act as a pattern for a new, identical strand of DNA. This discovery opened up a brand-new field of science: genetics.

DID YOU KNOW?

James Watson, Francis Crick, and Maurice Wilkins were awarded the Nobel Prize in 1962 for their discovery of the structure and nature of DNA.

Dr. James D. Watson holds a model of DNA in 1957.

TRANSLATING
THE GENETIC CODE

Proteins do much of the work in a living thing. They fight disease, carry oxygen, help us move, and form body parts. They also run the chemical reactions that make our bodies work, such as digestion. There are thousands of proteins in our bodies, each with a **unique** and important job. The instructions to make those proteins are contained in areas of DNA called genes.

When a cell needs to make a certain protein, a copy of the gene in DNA is made into a molecule called messenger RNA. The messenger RNA then leaves the nucleus and "delivers the message" to ribosomes. Ribosomes are the protein factories of the cell. They translate the genetic code into amino acids, which are the building blocks of proteins.

14

KINDS OF RNA

RNA (ribonucleic acid) is very similar to DNA (deoxyribonucleic acid), except that DNA's nucleotides have one less oxygen atom. ("Deoxy-" means "less oxygen.") In addition, RNA has the base uracil rather than thymine. Like thymine, uracil binds to adenine. There are different kinds of RNA. Messenger RNA carries instructions that tell the ribosomes the order of amino acids. Transfer RNA transports the correct amino acids to help build the protein.

A microscope captures the action of RNA molecules attaching to DNA. Messenger RNA will be the result of the interaction.

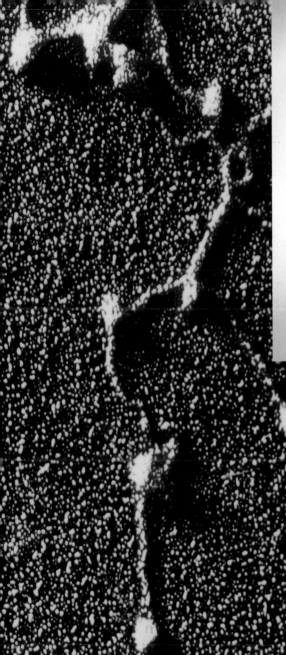

15

CRACKING THE CODE

Each codon has a three-letter name that corresponds to the names of its bases. Since there are only four bases in messenger RNA—adenine, uracil, cytosine, and guanine—codons use the letters A, U, C, G. There are 64 codons but only 20 amino acids. So more than one codon calls for a single amino acid. The codon that signals the beginning of the protein is AUG. There are several "stop" codons to signal the end: UAA, UAG, or UGA.

Transfer RNA recognizes each codon and adds the correct amino acid to the growing protein. Different kinds of transfer RNA are shown here in different colors.

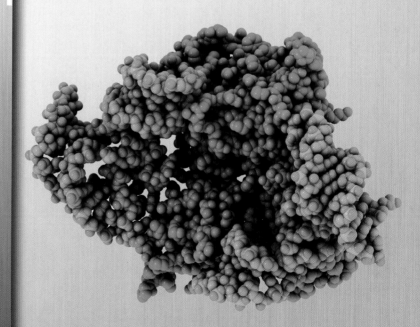

16

In the ribosome, the construction of a protein starts with messenger RNA. Messenger RNA contains bases grouped together in units called codons. Each codon is made up of three bases and corresponds to a certain amino acid. It's a bit like a secret code.

The ribosome reads each codon of the messenger RNA. Then transfer RNA goes to work. Its job is to match an amino acid to the codon. The ribosome then reads the next codon, and the transfer RNA places another amino acid. The ribosome attaches these two amino acids together. This is just the first step in building a protein. The cycle of reading codons and attaching amino acids repeats until the ribosome reads the codon that ends the protein.

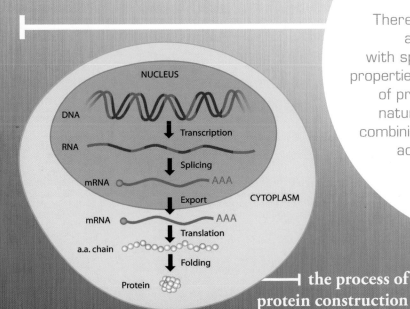

NUCLEUS

DNA

Transcription

RNA

Splicing

mRNA — AAA

Export — CYTOPLASM

mRNA — AAA

Translation

a.a. chain

Folding

Protein

the process of protein construction

17

LEARNING THE LANGUAGE

All living things contain DNA, and all DNA is made from the same four nucleotides. Even more amazing, nearly all living things—from bacteria to trees to humans—use the same codons when building proteins. Understanding the **sequence** of DNA nucleotides helps scientists and doctors better understand what we're made of, how our bodies work, and what genes cause diseases.

In the 1970s, Frederick Sanger mastered a **technique** for finding the sequence of DNA. He found a way to mark, or tag, nucleotides and add them to replicating DNA. The resulting sequence could be "read" because of these tags. Frederick Sanger won the Nobel Prize in Chemistry in 1980 for what is now called the Sanger Method.

DISTANT COUSINS

Genetically, people aren't that much different from other animals. We share about 44 percent of the same genes that fruit flies have and about 90 percent of the same genes mice have. Chimpanzees and humans share 98 percent of their genes. All humans have DNA that's about 99.9 percent similar to each other. No one has exactly the same DNA as another person, except identical twins, who receive the same DNA from each parent.

The technology of DNA sequencing has changed in the last 15 years. Long DNA sequences can now be figured out overnight by computers.

GENETIC DISEASE AND THE HGP

One of the goals of the Human **Genome** Project was to identify disease-causing genes. Cystic fibrosis is caused by a gene that tells the body to produce thick mucus in the lungs and digestive system. This leads to life-threatening infections and trouble absorbing nutrients. By studying the sequence of the responsible gene, researchers have a better understanding of the disease and have found new ways to treat it.

Printouts of DNA sequences often look like this. Scientists know how to "read" the sequence.

20

In 1990, the United States started the Human Genome Project (HGP). The goal of this undertaking was to identify all genes and sequence the nucleotides contained in human DNA. The genomes of other organisms, such as bacteria and mice, were also sequenced, so they could be compared to the human genome.

It wasn't long before other countries' scientists, including those from China, France, Germany, Great Britain, and Japan, contributed to the HGP. By April 2003, the HGP had completed its goals—more than 2 years ahead of schedule! It identified about 20,500 unique genes and published the sequence of 3 billion nucleotides found in human DNA. The information is free and available online for anyone to use.

DID YOU KNOW?

If the sequence of someone's DNA was printed out, it would fill 200 books, each containing 1,000 pages, and would take more than 9 years to read aloud!

Two scientists work to find the gene for a disease that causes blindness.

GENETICS AND ELECTRON MICROSCOPES

Light, or optical, microscopes can magnify an object up to 2,000 times. This might sound like a lot, but it's not enough to see DNA. **Electron** microscopes can magnify objects up to 2 million times! At this magnification, researchers can see individual strands of DNA and how they interact with other molecules, such as RNA and proteins.

The interaction of proteins and DNA is a major area of study in genetics. Special proteins, called transcription factors, control what's being copied onto messenger RNA. (Transcription is the process of copying.) Transcription factors bind to DNA near a gene and signal the cell whether or not to make a copy of that gene onto messenger RNA. Understanding how genes are turned on and off gives scientists insight into our bodies.

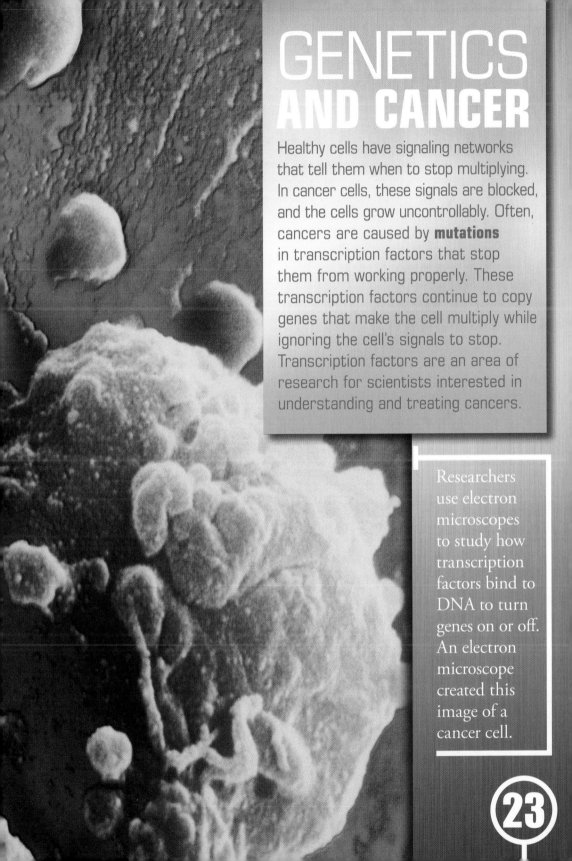

GENETICS
AND CANCER

Healthy cells have signaling networks that tell them when to stop multiplying. In cancer cells, these signals are blocked, and the cells grow uncontrollably. Often, cancers are caused by **mutations** in transcription factors that stop them from working properly. These transcription factors continue to copy genes that make the cell multiply while ignoring the cell's signals to stop. Transcription factors are an area of research for scientists interested in understanding and treating cancers.

Researchers use electron microscopes to study how transcription factors bind to DNA to turn genes on or off. An electron microscope created this image of a cancer cell.

23

TINY FACTORIES

Understanding genetics allows us to develop new tools and medications. For example, people with Type I diabetes don't make enough insulin, a **hormone** produced by the pancreas that controls the level of sugar in the blood. Without daily injections of insulin, some people could die. Starting in 1922, much of our insulin came from the pancreases of cattle or pigs. This was a costly and wasteful practice.

Since 1982, insulin has been produced safely and inexpensively. Scientists introduce the human insulin gene into bacteria and yeast. These microscopic organisms continuously produce human insulin as they grow. Amazing improvements like these have given people access to cheaper and more effective medications and have helped save animals' lives, too.

24

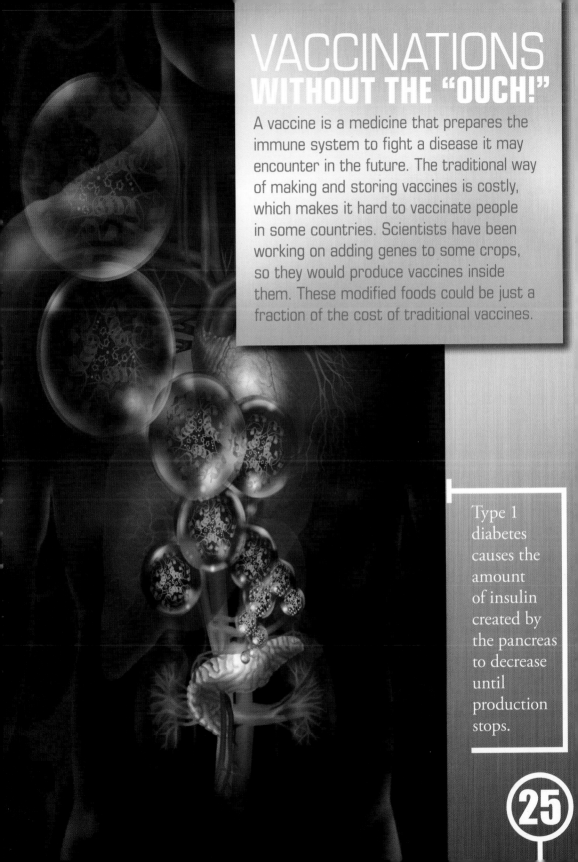

VACCINATIONS
WITHOUT THE "OUCH!"

A vaccine is a medicine that prepares the immune system to fight a disease it may encounter in the future. The traditional way of making and storing vaccines is costly, which makes it hard to vaccinate people in some countries. Scientists have been working on adding genes to some crops, so they would produce vaccines inside them. These modified foods could be just a fraction of the cost of traditional vaccines.

Type 1 diabetes causes the amount of insulin created by the pancreas to decrease until production stops.

25

FORENSICS

Forensics is the use of science and technology to help determine facts about a crime. An important part of modern forensics involves DNA. Extremely tiny amounts of DNA left at a crime scene can be recovered by specially trained people to find out whether a suspect was at the scene or not. In 1984, Alec Jeffreys discovered areas of DNA, called tandem repeats, that varied in length from person to person. Since then, many other techniques have been developed to analyze people's DNA, depending on how much is collected and how it's collected. Over the years, DNA has not only helped convict criminals guilty of serious crimes, but it has helped prove the innocence of those falsely accused.

WILDLIFE FORENSICS

Forensic scientists don't just investigate crimes against humans. The US Fish and Wildlife Service has a forensic laboratory dedicated to crimes against animals. Much of their work is similar to other crime labs, except they collect evidence from animals, such as fur, feathers, horns, and blood. They often focus on protecting at-risk species and preventing illegal hunting. The Wildlife Service Forensic Laboratory is the only one of its kind in the world.

Part scientist and part detective, forensic scientists are trained to look for clues so tiny that others may not notice them.

EVIDENCE BAG

Name/Rank/N

27

THE FUTURE OF GENETICS

DID YOU KNOW?

Some researchers study pharmacogenomics. In this science, DNA is examined to predict how a patient will respond to a medication.

As our knowledge of DNA and genes grows, so does the possibility of that knowledge helping us. Some diseases—such as cystic fibrosis—are caused by a single faulty gene. Researchers are studying the use of gene therapy (replacing a damaged gene with one that works correctly) as a way to treat or even cure these deadly diseases.

Our genes can make us more likely to have certain diseases like diabetes, cancer, or heart problems. Identifying those at high risk for certain diseases through DNA sequencing may encourage people to take healthy steps to lower that risk, such as eating healthy foods and losing weight. Spotting and treating these diseases earlier can often help save lives.

FROM GENE TO PROTEIN:
HOW DNA WORKS

DNA contains all the information necessary for life.

Transcription factors bind to DNA, which signals DNA to copy a gene to messenger RNA.

The messenger RNA is transported to ribosomes, where genetic code is translated into amino acids. Transfer RNA brings the correct amino acids to ribosomes.

The amino acid chain continues to grow until a stop codon is reached. The protein is released.

Some proteins, like transcription factors, stay in the cell and keep it running properly.

Others, like insulin, are transported outside the cell to be used throughout the whole body.

ETHICS OF DNA

Most people would consider using genetics to cure a disease a good thing. But what about using genetics to make children more intelligent, taller, or faster? Should someone not be hired for a job because their DNA suggests they have a high risk for a disease that would make them miss work in the future? As a society, we must think about these and similar questions as we step into the future.

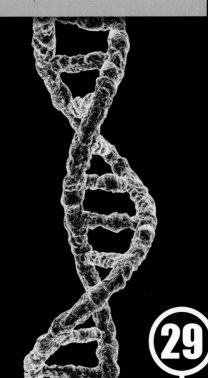

29

GLOSSARY

bacteria: tiny creatures that can only be seen with a microscope

electron: a tiny particle in atoms. An electron microscope uses a beam of electrons to create an image of a microscopic object.

genetic: relating to genes

genome: the complete set of all DNA in an organism

hormone: a chemical made in the body that tells another part of the body what to do

mutation: a change in a gene

nutrient: something a living thing needs to grow and stay alive

resolution: the ability of a microscope to make it possible for people to see parts of an object or objects close to each other

sequence: in genetics, the particular order of nucleotides in DNA or RNA

technique: a method or skill used in a particular task

trait: a feature that is passed on from parents to children

unique: being the only one of its kind

X-ray: a powerful type of energy that is similar to light but is invisible to the human eye

30

FOR MORE INFORMATION

BOOKS

Johnson, Rebecca L. *Amazing DNA*. Minneapolis, MN: Millbrook Press, 2008.

Walker, Richard. *Human Body*. Boston, MA: Kingfisher Publications. 2006.

WEBSITES

The Basics on Genes and Genetic Disorders
kidshealth.org/teen/your_body/health_basics/genes_genetic_disorders.html
Find out more about how genes and diseases can be passed down through families.

Genetics
www.neok12.com/Genetics.htm
Watch short videos of many basic concepts of genetics.

How DNA Works
science.howstuffworks.com/environmental/life/cellular-microscopic/dna.htm
Read more about DNA, and check out links to find out how forensics works.

INDEX

adenine 6, 7, 10, 11, 13, 15, 16

amino acids 14, 15, 16, 17, 29

base 6, 10, 12, 13, 15, 16, 17

chloroplasts 11

chromosomes 8, 9

CODIS 26

codons 16, 17, 18, 29

Crick, Francis 12, 13

cytosine 6, 7, 10, 11, 13, 16

deoxyribose 6

DNA sequencing 18, 19, 20, 21, 28

double helix 6, 7, 12, 13

electron microscopes 22, 23

forensics 26, 27

Franklin, Rosalind 12

genes 14, 18, 19, 20, 21, 22, 23, 24, 25, 28, 29

gene therapy 28

genetics 13, 22, 24, 29

genome 21

guanine 6, 7, 10, 11, 13, 16

Human Genome Project 20, 21

karyotype 9

messenger RNA 14, 15, 16, 17, 22, 29

mitochondria 11

mitochondrial DNA 11

mutations 23

nucleotides 6, 7, 10, 12, 13, 15, 18, 21, 22

nucleus 4, 5, 8, 11, 14

pharmacogenomics 28

phosphate 6

proteins 11, 14, 15, 16, 17, 18, 22, 29

ribosomes 14, 15, 17, 29

RNA 15, 22

Sanger, Frederick 18

Sanger Method 18

tandem repeats 26

thymine 6, 7, 10, 11, 13, 15

transcription factors 22, 23, 29

transfer RNA 15, 16, 17, 29

uracil 15, 16

Watson, James 12, 13

Wilkins, Maurice 12, 13